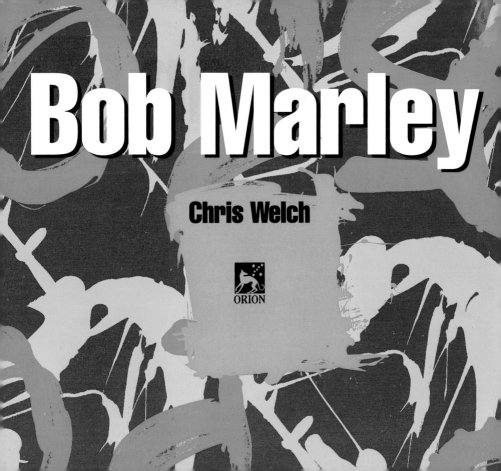

Bob Marley

Chris Welch

ORION

AN ORION PAPERBACK

This is a Carlton Book

First published In Great Britain in 1994 by Orion Books Ltd, Orion House, 5 Upper St
Martin's Lane, London, WC2H 9EA.

A CIP catalogue record for this book is available from the British Library.

ISBN 1 85797 328 3

Edited, designed and typeset by Impact Editions
Printed in Italy

THE AUTHOR

Working on a wide experience of music papers and magazines, Chris Welch has a
reputation as a respected journalist. He has written about and championed many
artists, including Genesis and Jimi Hendrix. He currently edits *Rock World Magazine*.

Contents

Bob Marley
20th Century Prophet

Was he a prophet? A leader of men with a divine mission and mysterious powers? Or was he only (only!) a brilliantly-gifted singer, songwriter and performer who represented the fight for freedom for millions in the Third World? Depending on your viewpoint both answers are equally true. But then confusion surrounded Bob Marley in his life, why should it be any different now? Here are two examples of Marley's duality of experience:

In December 1976, Bob Marley appeared in Jamaica in front of 50,000 people in the "Smile Jamaica" concert.

play his guitar.

The intention of the concert had been to emphasize the need for peace in Kingston's ghettoes, but the local gangsters had got to Bob Marley first—the consequences could have been tragic.

On April 18, 1980, the African country formerly known as Rhodesia declared its independence under a new name—Zimbabwe. Bob Marley and the Wailers were invited to play at the Independence Ceremony, an enormous honour for a group of musicians who'd grown up in the slums of Jamaica. Even so, as they performed in front of new Prime Minister Robert Mugabe and royal guest Prince Charles, Bob Marley was experiencing doubts about his political and religious beliefs. Outside the Rufaro Stadium in Salisbury, police were using tear-gas to control the crowds. Some of the gas billowed across the stage, and as Marley should have been enjoying his

"My music will go on forever!"

It was a gesture of defiance for Bob to do the 90-minute set—only days earlier, he had been shot in the arm as part of an assassination attempt, and had to perform without being able to

"Music don't care...music just wants be. All you have to do is make sure them things in tune, 'cause when it don't tune, music vex."
Bob Marley 1980

proudest moment, police were having to fire over the heads of the crowd to prevent an unruly mob from breaking into the arena. There was a growing realization in Marley's mind that the newly-liberated crowd wasn't really listening to his music—or his message. Yet for Marley, that message was all-important...

Marley Magic

In an epoch that saw the impact of many exciting, productive artists, from Bob Dylan to Jimi Hendrix, the contribution of Bob Marley and the Wailers shook up a world that thought it had grown used to revolutions. The reggae music they espoused became a clarion cry for the peoples of the Third World, while still being embraced by the mass audience for rock and pop as an hypnotic, intriguing new musical force.

The story of how a young man from the West Indies became a global star, and achieved huge commercial

Jimi Hendrix shared Marley's interest in things magical. He wrote 'Voodoo Chile' for an African healer.

success while maintaining an almost mystical, religious status, has been a constant source of fascination ever since Marley's tragic death. Few rock stars could claim to have had so much influence, or to have led such an extraordinary life, marked as it was with intrigue, danger and mystery.

A charismatic performer and a challenging public figure, his roots lay in the street culture of Jamaica, and the ethos of Rastafarianism. But it wasn't until his work was brought to the attention of the outside world with the marketing experience of the rock industry, that Bob Marley and the Wailers became household names. Such albums as *Catch A Fire* and hit songs 'I Shot The Sheriff' and the tender 'No Woman No Cry' caught the public's imagination on a scale that had rarely been achieved by the earlier reggae pioneers.

The folk memory of slavery remained a constant factor in Jamaican life, and this gave Marley's lyrics a substance and power that went far beyond the trivialities of most rock and pop songs. The need for redemption, a messiah, and freedom lay at the heart of a movement that offered an alternative to oppression.

But while Marley's music and life were devoted in many respects to a religious search, he was surrounded by the realities of a violent world from which he would eventually have to escape.

His own beliefs and philosophies were full of contradictions and inconsistencies, but faith remained the key. Whether you believed in Rastafarianism and the potent religious symbol of Jah or not, and whether Marley himself believed it all, was irrelevant.

There were years when Marley's memory faded as reggae itself went into the doldrums, with black American culture re-asserting its dominance through new musical forms, from hip-hop to rap. But ten years on there has

been a huge resurgence of interest, fuelled by the issue of Island Records' commemorative boxed set.

Revered by millions of followers, the victim of a terrifying assassination attempt, honoured by his country after his death from cancer on May 11, 1981—Marley is one of the few artists to have truly earned the title bestowed on the tribute album to Robert Nesta Marley... *Legend*

Left: "Them belly full, but we hungry!"

Bringing the message of Jah to the people.

The Marley Mystery

When Bob Marley first made an impact on the consciousness of international audiences in the early Seventies, he seemed to epitomize the street-wise, ganja-smoking, Rastafarian rebel. With his alarming natty dreadlocks, and heavy use of impenetrable Patois—the deconstructed Jamaican version of the English language—Marley and his disciples seemed an exotic breed. But years later it was revealed that Marley came from a surprising family background, and a fascinated public were amazed to learn that not only was his father a white man, but he was an officer in the British Army.

Robert Nesta Marley was born in Rhoden Hall, in the north of Jamaica. His mother was an 18-year-old black girl, Cedella Booker, known as Ciddy, and his father was Captain Norval Sinclair Marley, a 50-year-old quartermaster attached to the British West Indian Regiment. He had been a superintendent for the Crown lands, and it was his job to encourage

Bunny Livingstone, Marley's childhood friend, played soccer in the "Yards" before he played guitar in The Wailers.

resettlement and farming deep inside the country. Although he stood accused of having seduced a country girl much younger than himself, and both would suffer censure and criticism as a result, he stood by Cedella and the couple were married in June 1944. Their son Robert was born on February 6, 1945. Given the state of relations between black and white races during those years, it's not surprising that there was family pressure on Captain Marley. He was disinherited and denounced and he gave up his job to return to Kingston for a less-demanding post. But this meant he rarely saw his son while young Robert was growing up in the rural area of St.Ann. The Captain provided financial support, and later arranged for him to move to the capital, but at first the wife and son were left to live in a one room shack.

Ciddy was left to bring up her son and support him by running a grocery store. She also worked in the fields

Soccer was Bob Marley's passion from schooldays to superstar days.

and Robert was required to help by carrying water pails and messages to the workers. One of his earliest school

"When I lived in the ghetto, every day I had to jump fences, police trying to hold me. So I don't want to stay in contact with the ghetto."
Bob Marley 1979

friends acquired during these not unhappy childhood days was Neville "Bunny" Livingstone (born April 10, 1947). They would sit together during story-telling time listening to the village elders, hearing tales of myth, magic, and "black heart mon," the bogeyman of local legend. Inevitably, there were tales too about Haile Selassie, the Emperor of Ethiopia, the black king from Africa who was regarded with great awe and respect and who, it was said, would one day lead all Africans to their true homeland. Such tales were to spark a life-long fascination in Marley both with the the mysteries of magic and the Emperor who played such an important part in a cult known as Rastafarianism that had since spread throughout Jamaica.

As a very young child Marley

"When I started singing, I remember hearing Jamaican singers getting popular—like Jimmy Cliff." said Marley.

Singing songs of Trench Town, the birthplace of reggae, rudeboys and Rastas.

developed a talent for palm reading and fortune telling that would earn him a reputation as an "Obeahman" or mystic among neighbours and his family. They were impressed by his psychic powers and a strange presence, enhanced by a penetrating gaze that made even older people uncomfortable. But in all other respects, he was a normal child.

Lost boy

When he was five years old Robert went to the local Stepney School. Then in 1950 he was sent to Kingston at the behest of his absent father, supposedly for a better life and education than could be obtained deep in the country. But in a bizarre twist of events, his mother lost track of her son from the moment he arrived in the big city. It seems he was taken

away by Captain Marley and left with an elderly woman who was to look after him. There was no word from either father or son. Both had vanished into the teeming streets of Kingston. It was several months before his mother tracked down Robert with the help of friends, and returned him to their home in the country. There was no explanation for the Captain's behaviour except that it seemed he preferred his son to be brought up as an orphan. Later Cedella's estranged husband would bigamously remarry, yet despite protests, the authorities would take no action against him. However Captain Marley had suffered from ill health for years and a few months later, on May 20, 1955, he died from a heart attack, leaving Cedella and Robert to fend for themselves.

It was decided to try a return to Kingston and this time the plan was that mother and son would eventually be together. Cedella went first, and got

Left: When Peter "Tosh" McIntosh met Bob and Bunny he shared their dreams of stardom.

Bob contemplates his roots and the history of Jamaica.

a job working as a cook, while living in rented accommodation in one of the "Yards," the grim and basic housing schemes provided by the Government. Robert was left in the care of friends and relatives until he proved too unruly, and was sent on a bus with his friend Bunny Livingstone, to be reunited with his mother.

At the age of ten he was packed off to a private school, rather than one of the ghetto establishments which were considered breeding grounds for crime. Low expectations and unemployment meant that many Jamaican youths were prone to self-doubt and violence, unless they were offered a way out. Inevitably they became hardened to ghetto conditions, and Robert Marley saw his school friends transformed from innocent kids into "rude boys" whose lives revolved around robbery, fighting and gang culture.

Life in the Yards was grim, but it offered a sense of "belonging" to which Bunny and Robert quickly adapted, as they learnt the rules:

How to play football, how to play cards and how to use a knife...

As the boys were growing up in these conditions, outside forces were beginning to take effect on their homeland. Music, politics and religion would combine to transform their society. For the young, it was music that provided the most enjoyable diversion from ghetto life. The arrival of the transistor radio in the late Fifties meant that Jamaican kids could tune into the R&B music being broadcast from the States, and they enjoyed hearing the rocking hits of Fats Domino and Louis Jordan. There were also the local blues dances, presided over by the legendary DJ, Sir Coxsone, who used a giant sound system to blast out records at full volume.

It wasn't long before local boys began to make their own records and create their own jukebox hits. The seeds of the Jamaican music scene were being sown.

Star dreams

Robert Marley sang like the American crooners and his friend Bunny played a home-made guitar while they imagined themselves becoming stars. They were taking their first hesitant steps towards a musical career. Certainly being a singer and musician was a much more attractive option than becoming an apprentice welder, which was the job his mother had him lined up for at the age of 15.

Robert and Bunny were fascinated by the music they could pick up from

> **"My father was a white guy, my mother was black woman, and I came in between. Like, you know, I'm nothing. All I have is God."**
> *Bob Marley 1977*

As a child, Marley was alarmed by the sight of Rastafarians in their dreadlocks!

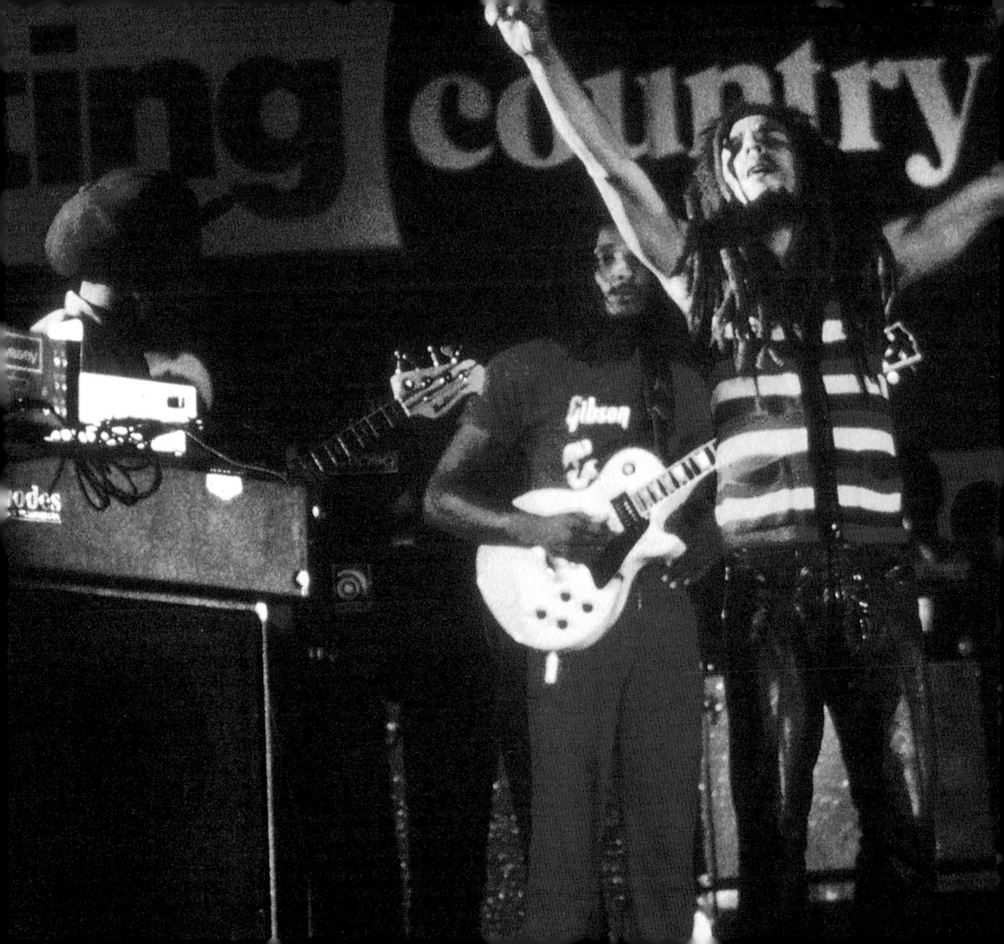
ing
Gibson

the American stations. In particular there was one New Orleans station that broadcast the latest tunes by Ray Charles, Curtis Mayfield and Brook Benton. Bob and Bunny also paid close attention to the black vocal groups, like the Drifters, who were extremely popular throughout Jamaica.

When Bob finally quit school, his main ambition was unquestionably to go into music, although to please his mother he got a job in a welding shop. Nevertheless Bob spent all his free time with Bunny, perfecting their vocal skills. They were helped by the singer Joe Higgs, who held informal lessons for the aspiring vocalists in the tenement yards. It was at one of these sessions that Bob and Bunny met Peter McIntosh, another youth who had big musical ambitions.

By 1962 Bob Marley had

Fiery preaching would be greeted with alarm by the Establishment.

One day Bob Marley would receive his country's third highest honour, Jamaica's Order Of Merit.

auditioned for a local music entrepreneur called Leslie Kong. Impressed by the quality of Bob's vocals, Kong took the singer into the studio to cut three sides, the first of which called 'Judge Not' was released on the Beverly label. It was Marley's first record. Two other tunes 'Terror' and 'One Cup Of Coffee' were also released, but didn't receive any airplay. At least the exercise confirmed Marley's ambition—to be a singer.

Early influences

The young Robert Marley had been interested in history at school, and in particular in his country's colonial past.

"Music is a dangerous game. A musician man is a man him soft in him heart. Him slightly different."
Bob Marley September 1975

He was also fascinated by the Back to Africa movement begun early this century by the Reverend Marcus Garvey, a movement which later turned into Rastafarianism once Jamaicans had identified Emperor Haile Selassie as the black king who would bring about their redemption (see Appendix 1).

However for the moment he was a child growing up in the Fifties; a time when the country folk of Jamaica were pouring into town, only to end up living in shanty towns on the outskirts. The most notorious was Trench Town to the west of Kingston, named after the drainage ditch over which it was built.

When Bob Marley and his mother moved into Trench Town in the late Fifties it was because of a desperate need to better themselves. Cedella knew that life there would be tough and unpleasant, but there was always a chance that the family might be able to save enough money to move to America or England.

Into the melting pot

I n September 1959 the Jamaica Broadcasting Corporation went on the air and began sponsoring local talent with live shows and contests. When they introduced their own hit parade charts, it was a great boost to the music scene and encouraged a burgeoning homegrown record industry. The station had its own single-track studio and the station was deluged with guitar players and singers eager to get on air.

Jamaica had long been a melting pot of musical ideas, as players were influenced by a curious mixture of European classical and folk music, African drumming and American R&B. Between the wars the most popular local music was called Mento and was

Georgie Fame pioneered an authentic sounding British version of ska and bluebeat in London.

Right: Millie Small pioneering bluebeat and ska music in Britain.

based on a syncopated rumba beat.

This was later supplanted by the calypso, the cheerful mixture of topical themes set to a lively rhythm. Calypso became very popular in America and England and one of the biggest hits was 'Rum And Coca Cola' which was covered by the Andrews Sisters.

When Mento was partially revived in the early Sixties in the hope of appealing to tourists, it was greeted with interest by a new generation of players. They mixed it up with R&B and the result was a new musical form known as ska, based on the 12-bar shuffle blues.

The ska craze spread to London where it was called bluebeat. It was played in West Indian clubs, but local white teenagers, the Mods, adopted the music too, and it was played by such bands as Georgie Fame and the Blue Flames at Soho's Flamingo Club. The biggest bluebeat hit though was by Millie whose 'My Boy Lollipop' was released by Anglo-Jamaican

As the sound systems grew in size and popularity, so too grew the rivalry between dance organizers and the DJs—known as toasters. Among the most famous of these were Duke Reid and Coxsone Dodd (as a school cricket player he was nicknamed "Sir Coxsone" after an English cricket star). He had brought the concept of the high-powered sound system to Jamaica after working for a while in the States. He had been to outdoor dances where R&B records were blasted out at full volume. He employed amateur boxer Prince Buster, and Lee Perry, as talent scouts to find new recording artists, entrepreneur Chris Blackwell.

The local Jamaican radio station wasn't too receptive to the new music so the alternative was to play it on the sound systems. As American R&B had become watered down, so there was a need for a stronger, harder dance beat, which the local ska musicians could supply.

Left: The Wailing Wailers, as sharp young Mods, seen here in 1965 with (left to right), Bunny Livingstone, Bob Marley and Peter Tosh.

> **"If God had no given me a song to sing, I wouldn't have a song to sing. The song comes from God, all the same."**
> *Bob Marley June 1976*

Desmond Dekker, pioneer reggae star, used to sing with Bob when both were learning a trade in a welding shop.

and act as unofficial bodyguards. Protection was vital in order to ward off the attentions of rivals who would try to steal the takings from dances and even wreck the equipment.

Soon the records made for the sound system DJs would be pressed up for the commercial market and against all expectations, sold in huge numbers, as the ska dance craze took off. Among the early artists to make a name for themselves were Jackie Edwards, and Laurel Aitken. It was still difficult for them to get adequate airplay, but the sound systems ensured the records would become huge hits, and the singers and bands began to pack out local venues. Then one day a Jamaican record, 'Rock Boogie' by Laurel Aitken, became JBC's number one chart record and

the population was astounded and delighted.

Ska and bluebeat dominated Jamaican music throughout the early Sixties, and it wasn't until 1968 that the next development, reggae would emerge.

In the autumn of 1961 Bob Marley, aware of all these early developments, with his first three songs already written, and encouraged by a neighbourhood friend Desmond Dekker had gone in search of Coxsone Dodd at the Federal Studios. Instead he met producer Leslie Kong at the front door, and another aspiring young singer/songwriter called Jimmy Cliff.

Marley was ordered to sing a song to the producer without any accompaniment, but passed this

Peter Tosh, a tall swaggering youth, wanted to take charge of the Wailers, but Robert Nesta Marley was their natural leader.

difficult test and was sent straight into the studio to record his three compositions including 'Judge Not', 'Terror' and 'One Cup Of Coffee', with a backing band of session musicians. He was paid just £20 (about $50) for the tunes and two acetate copies.

Some time later Marley would have an altercation with Kong and warned him that one day Kong would earn a lot of money from Marley—but he wouldn't live to enjoy it. It was an alarming example of Marley's ability to inspire foreboding and fear.

Being a recording artist was certainly much more fun, and more lucrative, than working as a welder repairing bicycle frames.

When 'Judge Not' was finally released, Marley played his own record on a local jukebox so many times that the weary owner finally removed the record from the machine, complaining it was giving him a headache!

One appalling incident finally

decided Marley on a full time career in music. He was hit in the eye by hot shards of metal while welding and was taken to hospital in agony to have the metal removed without anaesthetic. After this his mother promised he would never have to return to the work shop, although she was still wary of his wild ideas about being a professional musician and songwriter.

Dark, magical powers seemed to emanate from the singer who could predict people's fortunes—good and bad.

The Wailing Wailers

By now Marley was busy writing more material and decided that the best way forward was not to rely on session men for recording, but to form his own group. In the summer of 1963 he formed a vocal trio, first called the Teenagers and then the Wailing Wailers, with Bunny Livingstone and Peter McIntosh (who later shortened his surname to Tosh), together with singer Junior Braithwaite, and with Beverley Kelso and Cherry Smith as backing vocalists.

Robert was keen to improve their sound and encouraged Peter to get an acoustic guitar, which he borrowed

Violence at gigs was sometimes a problem in the early days, but Marley could usually get folks to simmer down.

"Name Wailers come from *The Bible*. There's plenty places you meet up with weeping and wailing. Children always wail, cryin' out for justice."
Bob Marley 1974

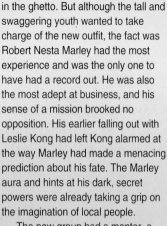

Lee "Scratch" Perry, production genius who virtually invented the sound of reggae.

from a church. As soon as he was armed with this, he liked to boast that he was the leader of the group.

Born in 1944, "Tosh" was an only child who had been raised by an aunt. After she died he lived with an uncle in Trench Town, and the teenager saw music as a way out of his dead end life

in the ghetto. But although the tall and swaggering youth wanted to take charge of the new outfit, the fact was Robert Nesta Marley had the most experience and was the only one to have had a record out. He was also the most adept at business, and his sense of a mission brooked no opposition. His earlier falling out with Leslie Kong had left Kong alarmed at the way Marley had made a menacing prediction about his fate. The Marley aura and hints at his dark, secret powers were already taking a grip on the imagination of local people.

The new group had a mentor, a Rastafarian hand drummer called Alvin Patterson, who at last introduced the youths to Sir Coxsone, the record producer in Kingston that Marley had most wanted to meet. Dodd auditioned the Wailing Wailers, liked what he heard, and agreed to record them.

After extensive rehearsals, coached and encouraged by Joe Higgs, the Wailers began recording such ska tunes as Marley's 'I'm Still Waiting'. On later sessions Marley turned up with a smaller outfit, because Junior Braithwaite was planning to leave Jamaica. Dodd insisted that they should have an identifiable leader and Bob Marley became the lead vocalist on a new song he'd written called 'Simmer Down', which was a piece of advice to the tearaway Rude Boys who were causing a major juvenile crime wave. Dodd brought in some top ska session musicians to play on the tracks including trombonist Don Drummond and Ernest Ranglin on guitar. The band itself had its own name, the Skatalites—in honour of the American and Russian space satellites that were beginning to circle the planet.

In 1966 Bob Marley married singer Rita Anderson, singer with the Soulettes. As Rita Marley she became the Queen of Reggae.

Simmer down

'Simmer Down', the Wailing Wailers' first single, was released on the Downbeat label in December 1963, and by the following February it was number one in the Jamaican charts, a position it held for the next two months. The new group was hot news and 'Simmer Down' caused a sensation when it sold a thousand copies a week. The Wailers began to record regularly for Coxsone Dodd's Studio One company. Their music identified with the Rude Boy street rebels of the Kingston slums and Jamaican music had found a tough, urban stance.

Over the next few years the Wailing Wailers would put out some 30 sides to establish them as one of the hottest groups in the country.

In the aftermath of 'Simmer Down', it was decided to release a ballad, 'It Hurts To Be Alone', and the Wailers were given an advance against royalties to buy themselves stage clothes as well as weekly wages.

The group made its live debut at a talent show at the Majestic Theatre in Kingston, when they covered Motown hits but also sang their own songs including 'Simmer Down', 'Hooligan', and 'Maga Dog'. In fact the Wailers didn't win the contest, Marley became involved in a fight with the winners and the police had to be called.

While Bob (as he now preferred to be called), was expanding his musical horizons his mother had other ideas of her own and wanted to move away from the dangers of Kingston, to Wilmington, Delaware, in the States where she had relatives. Eventually

Haile Selassie, Emperor of Ethiopia, became a hero figure to all Rastafarians.

"Life… It's life we deal with. No death. He that sees the light and knows the light shall live."
Bob Marley May 1973

Left: Under Lee Perry's direction Marley tightened up his vocal style and gave greater emphasis to the guitar.

Right: Getting into a reggae groove.

she remarried—Edward Booker, in Delaware in October, 1963.

Marley preferred to remain in the ghetto and the Wailers were kept busy through 1964 performing live shows and recording numerous singles including 'Mr. Talkative', 'I Don't Need Your Love', 'Lonesome Feelings' and 'Wings Of A Dove', many of which topped the charts.

But it was becoming financially difficult to hold the Wailers together and Junior Braithwaite and the two girl singers had since quit.

There was also the problem of violence at gigs, which culminated in fights at their Christmas show in Kingston. Then in the New Year the trombone player Don Drummond was arrested and charged with the murder of a dancer. The shock caused the break up of the Skatalites backing group and sent a tremor through the Jamaican recording scene.

Drummond was declared insane and sent to an asylum. The episode

"There should be no war between black and white!"

damaged the reputation of the whole music scene, but sensational press headlines and attacks only served to unite both musicians and the shanty town dwellers in their anger at the state oppression.

A new backing band, the Soul Brothers, was put together and they would go on to work with the Wailers on all their subsequent recordings for Dodd's labels.

In 1965 the Wailers issued a single called 'Rude Boy' at a time when civil rights leader Dr Martin Luther King visited the island, and when discontent in the shanty towns was at its height.

Meanwhile Cedella had saved sufficient money to send Bob an air ticket and the intention was for him to start a new life in the States. She wrote in the autumn of 1965 asking Bob to visit her in Delaware. But before he moved to America he proposed to his girlfriend Rita Anderson, a singer with the Soulettes. On February 10, 1966, they were married. Bob was 21 and Rita was 19. The day after the wedding Bob left her to fly to America.

Living in America

Marley's stay in America was short-lived. He worked just enough to finance his real ambitions which included setting up his own record label. He wanted to be free of Coxsone's musical direction for the Wailers and his insistence that they record unsuitable material.

Marley found the pace of life in the States far too fast and inhuman. But he did a variety of jobs, from driving a forklift truck to working as a waiter, an assembly line worker at Chrysler, and as a lab assistant.

Any free time he had was spent

An old guitar will never let you down.

Bob opened a window on the world.

Marley was hailed as a major poet and achieved a unique political power, as he was courted by his country's statesmen and leaders.

writing songs and playing his acoustic guitar. Rita flew out to see Bob and meet his family in August 1966. Then in October 1966, after eight months in America, he returned to Jamaica, having just missed the state visit by the Emperor Haile Selassie.

Bob would find himself increasingly drawn towards Rastafari, encouraged by the enthusiasm of Rita Marley, who had actually witnessed the visit of Haile Selassie. By the following year, 1967, his music reflected his new beliefs and he began to drop the Rude Boy anthems. In their place came a growing commitment to spiritual and social issues. By the mid-Sixties he would identify with the Rastafarians, began to grow

dreadlocks and smoke increasing amounts of ganja.

Meanwhile the Wailing Wailers had worked on during Bob's absence and their records had continued to sell—the fans were largely unaware that Bob was missing from the fold.

Marley joined up with Bunny and Peter to reform the group, now simply known as the Wailers, while Rita launched her own singing career, having a big hit with 'Pied Piper', a cover version of a current pop song. Musical trends were changing and the ska sound was being replaced by a slower rhythm called rock steady.

Marley had brought back around $700 (£500) from the States and opened a record shop which sold Coxone's releases and, excitingly, some on Marley's own label.

Because the Wailers' new commitment to Rastafarianism brought them into conflict with Coxsone Dodd, they were determined to control their own destiny and formed their record

> **"When people drink they want feeling I get when I smoke herb. Everybody need to get high, but some people getting high with the wrong things."**
> *Bob Marley June 1976*

label, called Wail' N' Soul' M after the Wailers and the Soulettes—their first two signings. They had a few successes, but it was hard work running a business as well as making music and the label folded in late 1967. For a while Bob went back to the land, working on a farm.

But he carried on writing. His group acted as songwriters for a company associated with the American singer Johnny Nash, who some years later would have a smash hit around the world with Marley's song 'Stir It Up'. In 1968 Nash (born Houston, Texas, 1940), had a hit called 'Hold Me Tight,' which he'd recorded at Federal

Robert Nesta Marley — a very special talent.

Studios. For some years Marley would pursue twin careers, writing for Nash and recording his own material.

Marley and the Wailers had now fallen out with Coxsone in a big way after a row at the studios between Coxsone, Peter Tosh and Bunny Livingstone, to which the police were called. Later the police would clamp down on the members of the band, arresting them on any pretext and having them sent to jail.

Bob himself spent two days in prison for a traffic offence. Against this background of official harassment, they recorded some more material with producer Leslie Kong, and also

> **"Money doesn't matter, music matters. When people think first about money... music won't be worth the money they were thinking about."**
> *Bob Marley 1977*

met up again with production genius Lee Perry, who it was claimed had virtually invented the pure sound of Jamaican music.

The birth of reggae

The Perry/Wailers combination resulted in some of the best records the band ever made. Tracks like 'Soul Rebel', 'Duppy Conqueror', '400 Years' and 'Small Axe' were classics that defined the direction of a new musical form that had begun to evolve called reggae.

Lee had worked for Coxsone and released a single directed at his old boss called 'The Upsetter'. Another single with a strange loping beat was called 'People Funny Boy'. This was later to be regarded as a forerunner of reggae. The new sound was soon endorsed by the Maytals who recorded a 1968 song called 'Do The Reggay', a reference to reggae's ragged, untidy beat.

But the new sound was hypnotic and addictive. The best exponents of this strange beat were brothers Carlton Lloyd Barrett (drums) and Aston "Family Man" Barrett (bass), who were the rhythmic nucleus of Lee Perry's studio band the Upsetters. The group had a big hit with 'Return

Goodbye Trench Town— hello rock 'n' roll.

45

Right: Marley and his coat of many colours.

Of Django' in the British charts in 1969 and the band visited the UK for a six-week tour during which they were given a warm reception. After the tour the Wailers asked them to support them on a song of Bob's called 'My Cup'.

They were unchallenged as Jamaica's hardest rhythm section and in 1970 they quit Perry and joined the Wailers. Perry was so furious he threatened to kill Bob Marley, but after a meeting it was agreed that Perry would become the Wailers' producer and the first result was a new song called 'Small Axe'.

As work under Perry's direction

proceeded, Marley improved and tightened up his vocal style, the backing vocals were given free rein and there was greater emphasis on guitar and less on horns.

The drumming was crucial to the new reggae sound and Carl Barrett developed a whole new approach, utilizing a heavy, nagging four beats on the bass drum, unexpected accents on his snare drum and a rattling fusillade on his hi-hat that was soon to be assiduously copied by drummers both black and white around the world.

The classic tracks like 'Duppy Conqueror' and 'Soul Almighty' were recorded during 1969 and the tapes were sent to England to be released by Trojan Records as Bob Marley and the Wailers' first album, titled *Soul Rebels*. It was released in the summer of 1970 in the UK and Jamaica with 'Duppy Conqueror' missing from the tracks.

The album sold well. Marley was

able to buy himself a car and repair his family home. His family now included two year old David "Ziggy" Marley and baby Cedella. As the family grew so Rita had to cut back on her own recording and look after their children, while Bob became ever more busy with the demands placed on a rising star.

'Duppy Conqueror' finally appeared on the band's second album *Soul Revolution* which was released on the Maroon label in 1971.

As inevitably happens when a band is successful, it was decided by the band's earlier producer, Leslie Kong, to bring out a *Best Of The Wailers* album consisting of repackaged versions of their early rock steady recordings. He was warned not to do it, but went ahead anyway. The album earned a lot of money, but Kong would not live to enjoy it. He died from a heart attack, aged 38. Marley's eerie prophecy had come true.

Catch A Fire

At the start of the Seventies Bob Marley and the Wailers were enjoying a huge reputation throughout the Caribbean but were still virtually unknown to the rest of the world. Marley's travels to Europe however were to create a growing interest in his work by both major and independent record companies.

In 1970 Bob accepted an invitation from Johnny Nash to accompany him to Sweden to work on a film score commission. The film was called *Want So Much To Believe* and Bob enjoyed life in Sweden, even though none of his songs were ever used in the film.

In 1971 he went on to visit London where he was welcomed by the immigrant community. He also signed a record deal with CBS and went into the studios to start recording material for Johnny Nash.

He called up his old friends in Jamaica and asked them over for a Wailers tour of Britain. They dutifully turned up and in the autumn played at some college gigs and London clubs like the Speakeasy, while helping out with the Nash recordings. Johnny's album, released on Epic and called *I Can See Clearly Now* featured three Marley compositions including one called 'You Poured Sugar On Me'.

The Wailers were supposed to be promoting a Marley single called

> "My music will go on forever. Maybe it's a fool say that, but when me know facts, me can say facts. My music go on forever."
> *Bob Marley June 1975*

48

Island Records' boss Chris Blackwell first saw major success for his label with Millie Small and her bluebeat chart buster 'My Boy Lollipop' back in 1964.

Marley got on well with Chris Blackwell, the Anglo-Jamaican head of Island Records.

been launched in Jamaica during the late Fifties. Blackwell, who had been impressed by the group's recent demo tapes, offered an £8,000 ($20,000) advance for the band to record a new album back in Jamaica.

It was a revolutionary move. For the first time a reggae band not only had access to the best recording facilities, but they were treated with the consideration usually accorded to a rock band.

Problems

Marley returned to the UK with the masters in 1972, to deliver them to Island. But there was a slight problem. Bob was already signed to CBS and a deal had to be struck for his release. Eventually Island got their album, which was called *Catch A Fire*. Overdubs were added in Island's London studios, utilizing the services of an American lead guitarist Wayne Perkins, who had never heard of reggae, and was alarmed by the

'Reggae On Broadway' but found themselves stranded in Britain.

In December Bob Marley walked into the Basing Street Studios of Islands Records and asked to see the label's founder, Chris Blackwell. The company had been one of the prime movers behind the rise of Jamaican music in Britain and had actually first strange appearance of the rastas. But he added some rock guitar to some of the tracks including 'Concrete Jungle'.

When *Catch A Fire* was released in April 1973 it received rave reviews in the rock press and was heralded as the harbinger of reggae—a new music that would sweep across the world. The album sold very well and plans were hatched by Blackwell to swiftly secure a follow up.

Gambling Man

Blackwell was just the man to work with and understand a complex character like Bob Marley despite his wealthy background (see Appendix 2). He knew Jamaica, was accustomed to the growing army of Rastafarians and could understand not only Bob Marley's patois but the convictions and

The Harder They Fall...when Jimmy Cliff flopped on Island Records, he left the way clear for Bob Marley & the Wailers.

Catch A Fire was the first reggae album packed with all the power of the rock business and its success set Marley's career alight.

beliefs that drove him.

Catch A Fire was the first album of all new material by a reggae band, previous albums being compilations of greatest hits and old singles. It was also beautifully packaged and heavily promoted. It meant the start of a long climb to fame and fortune.

Reggae poet Linton Kwesi Johnson later wrote about the album: "A whole new style of Jamaican music has come into being. It has a different character, a different sound… what I can only describe as International Reggae. It incorporates elements from popular music internationally: rock and soul, blues and funk. These elements

> "*Catch A Fire* was an introduction. Nobody knew who Bob Marley and the Wailers was. It was for people to get in and listen."
> Bob Marley 1974

facilitated a breakthrough on the international market." In fact Catch A Fire was not a huge hit, but it sold well enough and created the conditions for the band to tour.

Marley's hard dance rhythms, allied to his militant lyrical stance, came in complete contrast to the excesses of mainstream rock.

Island arranged for the Wailers to tour England and the States in 1973 to promote the album.

Marley and the band duly came to London in April, embarking on a club tour which hardened up the Wailers' act. They also appeared on BBC TV's The Old Grey Whistle Test, which included Bunny Livingstone playing percussion. But this was to be Bunny's last tour with the band—he couldn't stand the cold climates abroad and didn't like life on the road either. He returned to Jamaica and refused to play the American leg of the tour. He was replaced by Joe Higgs, the Wailers' original singing teacher.

Discovering a cache of herb? Actually it's a horde of Marley fans in the undergrowth at London's Crystal Palace.

When the band got to America Bob's mother Cedella, her husband Edward and their children, came from Wilmington to visit New York and hear the group play at Max's Kansas City. The band played three half-hour sets sharing the bill with a new young rock singer—Bruce Springsteen.

The band played to packed houses, and a 17-date autumn tour was arranged in which they would be supporting Sly and the Family Stone.

Four dates into the the the tour they played a concert in Las Vegas in October 1973 which caused a sensation. Most of the audience and the other bands were startled by the appearance of the Wailers and their charismatic lead singer, with his dreadlocks, fiery lyrics and pulsating "riddims." In fact they went down so well they were actually thrown off the tour for upstaging the headliners! The band went on to San Francisco where they broadcast a live concert for the rock radio station KSAN (the bulk of that session was finally made available in February 1991 when Island released the commemorative album *Talkin' Blues*).

Despite growing success there were rumblings of discontent within the Wailers at the way Bob was being promoted as the leader. Chief among those complaining was Peter Tosh who still thought he was the boss. It didn't seem to occur to them that all bands need a figurehead and nobody was better suited to the role than Marley. There were certainly rows with Lee Perry over the authorship of songs, and they almost came to blows when Perry claimed composer credits for Marley songs on a re-titled, reissued album called *Rasta Revolution*. Eventually they made it up, but the bitterness expressed by Tosh at the attention Marley was getting caused considerable personal hurt.

Heading Uptown

Back in Jamaica Marley moved into a big property called Island House in

When the Wailers made their American debut in 1973 they found themselves sharing the bill at Max's Kansas City club in New York, with a new young rock singer—Bruce Springsteen.

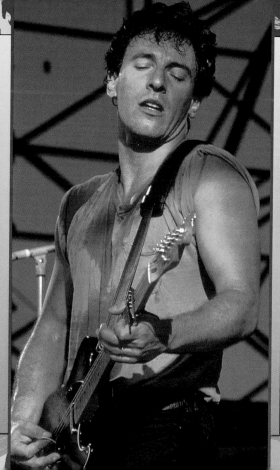

Dreadlocks flying, the charismatic reggae singer caused a sensation in Britain and America, as rock fans succumbed to the new music from Jamaica.

uptown Kingston, previously owned by Blackwell and which was to become his operational base, causing some jealousy among his older, less fortunate friends.

It was also a pleasant home for his growing family and there was no reason why Marley shouldn't enjoy some of the fruits of his labours. While there he spent his time jogging, playing soccer, smoking herb and discussing all the different aspects of Rastafari.

In 1973 the Wailers released their second Island album *Burnin'*, which included new versions of some of the band's older songs—such as 'Duppy

Conqueror', 'Small Axe' and 'Put It On' together with 'Get Up Stand Up' and 'I Shot The Sheriff' which Eric Clapton covered to achieve a Number 1 hit in the American singles charts.

With exciting songs like 'Burnin' And Lootin'' causing a furore, rock's royalty began to pay homage. Mick Jagger hired a reggae band to play at his wedding to Bianca, Keith Richards became a fan and Paul McCartney was also drawn to the music.

Marley himself began to be seen as a major Third World poet and was talked about in the same breath as statesmen and politicians. The Rastafarians had achieved some sort of political power, championed by the soon-to-be prime minister of Jamaica, Michael Manley, who visited Haile Selassie in Ethiopia to raise his own street credibility.

After Manley's election victory he took to visiting his near neighbour at Island House, the most famous citizen of Jamaica, Bob Marley.

> **"America is pure devilry the things that go on there. Them just work with force and brutality. Them lock out the punk thing."**
> *Bob Marley March 1979*

No Woman No Cry

In the following year Marley spent much of his time in the studio working on sessions that eventually yielded *Natty Dread* in 1974, an album that included such fiercely committed songs as 'Talkin' Blues', 'No Woman No Cry', 'So Jah Seh', 'Revolution', 'Them Belly Full (But We Hungry)' and 'Rebel Music (3 O'Clock Roadblock)'.

Bob Marley's house at 56 Hope Road, Kingston, Jamaica, was a far cry from the one-room shack that was his childhood home.

Rock stars paid homage to the new Third World music and Mick Jagger, always ahead of the latest trends, hired a reggae band to play at his wedding. Here's Mick on tour in 1973.

By the start of the next year, both Bunny and Peter Tosh had quit the group, feeling that they were being left out. A show by the original line up with the Jackson Five in Kingston in 1973 had been marked by tension within the Wailers. They would both embark on solo careers, while the band carried on as Bob Marley and the Wailers.

Tosh got a deal with CBS and went to New York to start recording. There was undisguised relief at his departure, because it meant an end to arguments and aggression at Island House. While the Wailers were touring however, Tosh suffered a severe beating at the hands of the police, as a warning against stirring up revolutionary fervour.

His response was to release a song called 'Legalise It' about herb, and it became one of Jamaica's biggest selling singles.

Natty Dread was released in February 1975 and by the summer the band went out on the road again. This time the harmony vocals usually provided by Bunny and Peter, were supplied by the I-Threes, a female trio comprising Bob's wife Rita, Marcia Griffiths and Judy Mowatt. Among the shows were concerts staged at London's Lyceum Ballroom, then a major rock venue. All who attended still recall Marley's Lyceum shows as highlights of the Seventies.

One of the Lyceum shows was recorded for a live album on July 18, 1975 and together with the single 'No Woman No Cry' both made a strong impact on the charts, as reggae music finally came out of the ghettoes and was placed firmly in the popular mainstream. By November, when the

Eric Clapton boosted Marley's reputation as a songwriter, when the guitar hero had a hit with Bob's 'I Shot The Sheriff'.

"What we black people really want is the right to be right, and the right to be wrong."
Bob Marley speaking out for black rights in June 1976

Keith Richards became a big fan of the Wailers, even lending Peter Tosh his Jamaican home—until Peter outstayed his welcome.

Wailers returned to Jamaica to play a benefit concert with Stevie Wonder, they were being hailed as the country's greatest superstars.

Earlier in the summer the Wailers and the I-Threes had toured the States with sold-out shows in San Francisco and at the Schaeffer Music Festival in New York's Central Park. After this Marley had been approached by Stevie Wonder and a joint show had been proposed. It was held in Kingston on October 11, 1975, with the proceeds scheduled to go to a blind school. Peter Tosh came back to the Wailers for the special event, and they played 'Rasta Man Chant',

"Me not of this world, y'know. Me live in the world, but I'm not of the world."
A spiritual Bob Marley reflects on the meaning of life in 1975

'Legalise It' and 'Battering Down Sentence'. Stevie Wonder played his own hits then launched into 'Boogie On, Reggae Woman' and invited the Wailers to jam with him. Then they played 'I Shot The Sheriff' with Stevie playing piano backing. It was an exciting moment and the show was hailed as a great cultural and musical triumph—but it was to be the last time that the original Wailers would ever play together.

Rita Marley and the I-Threes help spread the message.

Bad Vibes

After a friendly visit to Marley's home to smoke ganja, Tosh drove home with his girlfriend. Their car was hit head-on by another on the wrong side of the road. Tosh suffered severe facial injuries but his girlfriend Evonne died subsequently in hospital. After this tragic incident, Peter Tosh began to sever his ties with Marley.

Several months later the *Rastaman Vibration* album was released in 1976. This cracked the American charts and was the clearest example of Marley's musical philosophy. It included such tracks as 'Crazy Baldhead', 'Johnny Was' (about one of Trench Town's famed hoodlums), 'Who The Cap Fit' and 'War', the lyrics of which were

The I-Threes in action, with Bob's wife Rita Marley, Marcia Griffiths, and Judy Mowatt.

> **"Me love farming. Me wanna live on a farm later. Me no really wanna live in a flat and go to a club every night."**
> *Bob Marley*

taken directly from a speech by the Emperor Haile Selassie.

With the success of the new album, it seemed Bob Marley had taken over as the major superstar of the Third World.

While the lyrics seemed daring entertainment to Western rock fans, they had little idea of the sort of violence that was actually breaking out in Jamaica, where a State of Emergency was declared in June 1976. As the Wailers were setting off on their "Rastaman Vibration" tour, schools in Jamaica were being closed because of the danger of gunfire. There was also the complication of criminal elements trying to extort money from Marley, while rival political parties squabbled over his favours. In this hot-blooded, dangerous atmosphere Marley agreed to play a special free, outdoor show called "Smile Jamaica" sponsored by the Jamaican Ministry of Culture on December 5 at Kingston's National Heroes Stadium. The idea was to emphasize the need for peace in the city slums, where warring factions had brought turmoil and murder.

Just after the concert was announced, the Government called an election, to be held a few days later. The campaign was a signal for renewed ghetto war.

Bob was given protection by an armed guard but many of the Wailers were feeling too worried to concentrate on rehearsals. One of the singers, Marcia Griffiths, flew out of the country after having failed to persuade Bob to cancel the show. Marley himself had a nightmare about the sound of approaching gunfire. The nightmare was about to come true.

Marley offers his people the world.

"I know I was born with a price on my head."
Bob Marley expressing the fears of his own mortality in 1976

War!

Bob Marley was at the height of his fame, when the world was shocked to learn of a violent assassination attempt on him and his family and friends. Marley was shot in his home amid a hail of bullets fired by a mysterious gang of assailants armed with rifles and revolvers. It was probably the most frightening attack that any public entertainer had ever had to endure.

It happened in December 1976, during the run up to the "Smile Jamaica" concert and during a period when he was being threatened by a

Foreboding and fear gripped Marley on the eve of the attempt on his life by a gang of armed assassins. He was shot and injured in the attack in December 1976.

gang of extortionists. An election was due and there was already heightened tension in the shanty towns.

Island Records' boss, Chris Blackwell, was staying at a Kingston hotel where he met Bob's personal manager Don Taylor. Blackwell was feeling unwell and decided not to go, so Taylor visited Marley alone. Not long after he arrived, it was noticed that the armed guard that had been keeping watch on Island House had disappeared. As the occupants exchanged greetings shots were fired through the window, aimed at Marley. They hit Don Taylor instead and he fell bleeding to the kitchen floor. Although Marley was hit in the arm by one bullet, his life had been saved. At least two carloads of seven gunmen attacked the unguarded building, firing at random. Among those hit were Rita Marley—as she ran from the house with her children.

Mercifully no one was killed, but several of Marley's entourage were

seriously wounded and taken to hospital where they were met by Michael Manley. After treatment, Bob was driven under police escort to a camp in the mountains above Kingston where he was protected by

The singer found solace in family life as the pressures of fame began to build up.

Marley at an outdoor concert. In December 1976 he played at the Smile Jamaica concert, just after the failed assassination attempt.

Jamming with the Wailers.

soldiers and armed Rastafarians. The identities of the would-be assassins remained a mystery.

Said Marley about the incident later: "It kinda like this. Me there and then them come through the door and start gun shootin', blood claat! That mean I couldn't move. One time I moved to one side and the gunshot flew over, and then I moved this way and the gunshots go here.

"The feeling I had was to run hard, but God just moves me in time. His Majesty was directing me and as me moved me just feel like I get high. His Majesty, man he won't get me shot. But man it was dangerous. But it strengthened me, this experience. It hurt me on one arm, on one night, but me feel the vibes, me know something was going to happen. Me not know exactly what. One night I go to bed and in the night my vision say me in a barrage of gunshot, but me can't see

who fires the shot, and me like against the wall amid pure gunshot fire, but me not shot.

"When we me wake up, me start to think about me vision and realise it very serious vision, so me talk with the brethren about it. When I first heard gunshot outside, me jump and think to run, but I remembered the vision. In vision, don't run. I must stay, don't run.

I always knew I was born with a price on my head, but I don't know why I was shot. Maybe jealousy. Jealousy's a disease inside plenty people's brain. It stir 'em up and twist 'em round towards wickedness."

Bob was asked if he knew who had shot at him and he replied: "Yeah, but dat top secret. Really top secret. It was a miracle that me got saved. The whole thing was a miracle."

Despite very real fears that another attempt would be made on either

Every time I play, I get fresh inspiration.

Marley's or Michael Manley's life, it was decided to go ahead with the concert, and the Wailers played a powerful set to an audience of 50,000. Although Bob was unable to play his guitar because of his injury, he launched into a 90-minute set which opened up appropriately enough with 'War'. Rita Marley and Michael Manley watched, sitting on the top of a van for all to see. It was indeed a brave gesture of defiance.

A few days later Manley was victorious in the December 16 election when his PNP party captured most of the seats in the Jamaican House of Representatives.

Despite his political connections, Marley would later try to play down his involvement and distance himself from the politicians that Rastafarians believed were the main cause of the world's troubles.

Asked about the concert Marley said: "I said 'Smile, you're in Jamaica'. I didn't say 'Smile Jamaicans, be a

By the early Seventies Bob Marley was feted by rock society and almost deified as a god by his devoted followers.

After a heavy tackle during a game of soccer, Marley suffered a painful toe injury. "When I took off my shoe, the toe nail was completely out," he recalled later.

Jamaican'. I don't deal with that whole bag o' fuckery."

After the election Marley disappeared and the Kingston concert would be his last appearance in Jamaica for nearly 18 months. He left the country to visit his mother in Nassau, then went to America to recover his health in Miami. Next he flew secretly to England to live in London where he recorded his next album *Exodus*. His presence was revealed when he was fined for possession of cannabis.

At the same time he struck up a relationship with bands like the Clash and he identified with the punk movement because they seemed to be as much the butt of the

Marley touring on the Babylon bus.

Establishment as the Rastas. Bob would go into the studios to record a song about Rastas and punks with Aswad, an Anglo-Jamaica group, called 'Punky Reggae Party'. The song was later released on the Tuff Gong label.

Released in the summer, *Exodus* helped establish the band's international status. The album

"Jah appear to me in a vision."

stayed in the UK charts for 56 weeks, and three singles 'Exodus', 'Waiting In Vain' and 'Jamming' were all big hits. The title track was the first to receive heavy air play on black radio stations in America. The song was all about leaving Babylon in an exodus of Jah people to their forefather's land in Africa.

Bob was asked if the album's sound was different because it was recorded in England, and he told a reporter: "No, we're all on it right? And it's roots music, so if one man get too giddy, the other all seh 'Hey, him gettin' giddy!' I mean him (guitarist Junior Marvin) get too psychedelic and the islands don't like that, not a giddy man."

As reggae began to influence and be taken up by bands in England including the Police and the Clash, many wondered whether Marley would be resentful. In fact he didn't seem to mind that the style was being adopted and spread around.

> **"The more people smoke herb, the more Babylon fall."**
> *Bob Marley with another insight into the smoking of ganja, this comment coming in February 1976*

"I hear 'Police And Thieves', you know dem Clash. And I hear some more. Reggae music is a feeling, but reggae music is not the first time that feeling come on to the earth. That feeling is always there with the people, black and white. Even with ordinary people who no make no music. I hear the Police do something one time and I figure it kinda nice. It's not Jamaica it's coming from, but it still sound good.

"I don't care what people do with the music. Every time I play, I get fresh inspiration. It fresh, and no one can hear a song that you write until it come out on a record. So people can

"Babylon is gonna fall!"

capitalize on reggae as much as they want. We can play different music from the kind of music we play now. So if someone try to catch up with us, we can leave and change again, because that's what we've been doing over the years. Every time we make some music and they catch up with us, so we change, just like ska, rock steady and reggae. If them come too much and call it reggae, we go to Nyahbingi music, the first music. It mean 'death to black and white oppressors'. That type of music come from the heart. Every time you hear it, some time soft, sometime frightening, you get to know it. Like when I first hear rasta drumming, I think something terrible going to happen, because it's something we no understand. Reggae is a music that has plenty fight. But only the music should fight, not the people. Reggae doesn't have to be political or angry. It can be about anything. Most things are worth making music about."

Marley thought the actual term reggae came from a Spanish word, meaning "king music", but whatever its origins he was proud of his part in its development.

"Reggae is what you call international music, complete music. Any music you want play inside of reggae, you can put it here. Proud rhythm, that can't end. It's like from the beginning of time, from creation."

During their 1977 trip to England the Wailers played a week of concerts at London's Rainbow Theatre, which would be their last dates in the city during the Seventies.

In America the unlikely pop hero was feted by the stars and record company bosses, but even as he was lionized by rock society, he seemed to be increasingly distracted. While playing football with a French team in May 1977 during the "Exodus" tour he injured his right toe (for a second time). For some reason the injuries would not heal, and he was in some pain as he continued his Scandinavia tour dates.

Said Bob: "In Paris I was playing soccer and a man gave me a ras-claat tackle in the rain. The foot started paining me and I wonder now why it kept burning for so long. I scored a goal and just hopped off the field. When I took off my shoe, the toenail was completely out."

Worries began to grow among his friends about the state of his health. When he got back to London a limping Marley was taken by an Island Records executive to see a doctor, who found the injured toe was in such a bad condition he recommended that

Bob's son Ziggy Marley, was a member of the Melody Makers when he was 11.

"I don't eat meat, but it's easy, a Bible tell you what to do—mustn't eat pork, mule, horses, donkeys, duck, but you can eat fowl."
Bob on religion and health in 1976

> "Me don't want fight no guy with no guns, me musn't fight for my rights, my rights must come to me. You stand up for your right."
> *Bob Marley 1975*

Stevie Marley was a Melody Maker when he was five.

it should be amputated. But Bob refused on the grounds that such surgery was against Rastafarian laws. He was flown from London to Miami to see a black surgeon who carried out a skin graft instead. But instead of being cheered by the apparent success of the operation he privately confided to friends that he felt a strange feeling that he didn't have long to live.

One Love Peace Concert

In 1978 the band capitalized on their chart success with the next album *Kaya* which hit Number 4 in the UK the week after its release. The album saw Marley in a completely different mood,

singing a collection of love songs and homage to the power of ganja. There were two chart singles from the album 'Satisfy My Soul' and the beautiful 'Is This Love'.

There were a number of major events in Marley's life in 1978. He was invited to the United Nations in New York to receive the organization's Medal of Peace, presented at a special ceremony by the Ambassador from Senegal. At the end of the year he also visited Africa for the first time, going initially to Kenya and then on to Ethiopia, the spiritual home of the Rastafari. There he was shocked to see the same kind of poverty and oppression that he experienced all his life in Jamaica.

He was also deeply disturbed to discover that in Ethiopia Haile Selassie, the man who Marley thought was a God, had died in disgrace and was buried in an unmarked grave. There were no memorials to him and it seemed the Ethiopian people had no

respect for the black Emperor. It gave Marley much food for thought.

It was also in 1978 that the band toured Europe and America, doing a series of shows that provided a second double live album *Babylon By Bus* with material recorded during a concert in Paris in June.

The Wailers also broke new ground, playing in Australia, Japan and New Zealand, finally proving that reggae music truly did have international appeal.

But perhaps the most important event was to come in April when he returned to Jamaica to play the One Love Peace Concert …

Return To Jamaica

The year had begun with Marley flying back to Jamaica on February 26, where he was met by a crowd of 2,000 at the airport. It was his first trip back since the attempt on his life. He had been asked to return home specifically to appear at the One Love Peace

Concert which was to be held on April 22. It was organized by rival political parties with the aim of raising money for the poor, and also to rescue the country from the brink of civil war. The economy was in a state of collapse and Jamaica desperately needed the kind of unity only a figure like Bob Marley could provide.

A Jamaican Peace Movement had been set up after a series of political killings, and the country's top reggae acts had agreed to appear at the concert. Unfortunately just before the concert, some peaceful protesters in a slum area were killed by security police.

It seemed all the good work for peace might be in vain, but the concert went ahead and Marley even managed to get rivals Prime Minister Michael Manley and Leader of the Opposition Edward Seaga up on stage during a version of 'Jamming'. This appearance was at first greeted by silence, and then by cheers. The release of *Kaya* with its many love songs, coincided with this significant event, but there were still far too few signs of peace in Jamaica as the violence continued.

Survival

The next year, in 1979, the Melody Makers were formed (taking their name from the British weekly music newspaper). The group consisted of four of Bob and Rita Marley's children: Sharon (14), Cedella (12), Ziggy (11), and Stephen (5). They released a song by Bob and Rita called 'Children Playing In The Street' and the proceeds went to the UN Children's Fund during the International Year of the Child.

Survival, Marley's ninth album for Island Records was released in the summer. It included 'Zimbabwe' a stirring anthem for the new nation emerging from Rhodesia. Other tracks included 'So Much Trouble In The World', 'Ambush In the Night' and 'Africa Unite'.

Bob's daughter Cedella Marley, named in honour of his mother.

> **"People rob me and try to trick me, but now I have experience. Now I don't get tricked. Used to make recordings and not get royalties."**
>
> *Bob Marley June 1976*

The sleeve design comprised the flags of the independent nations, which showed that *Survival* was intended to support Pan-African solidarity.

Bob previewed two of the songs from *Survival* at a concert at the National Heroes Arena for Rasta children on September 24, 1979. One of them, 'Ambush In The Night' was about the attempt on his life, and the other was 'Zimbabwe' which showed the strength of his commitment towards similar freedom to be bestowed on Jamaica.

At the start of the new decade, Marley was honoured around the world as not merely a major reggae star, but a revered figure-head and spokesman for his people. As one American media boss crassly put it: "You're bigger than Christ and Muhammad combined!"

But such fame earned him many enemies, and it was even rumoured that the CIA, as well as political foes, were out to get him. His increasingly pro-Marxist views were not welcome during the cold war climate of the early Eighties.

Early in 1980 Bob Marley and the Wailers flew to Gabon, where they were to make their African debut. It was not quite the occasion that Marley was hoping for because the band discovered they were playing to the country's young elite, rather than the poor. Nevertheless they made a quick return to Africa, this time at the official invitation of the Government of the newly liberated Zimbabwe to play at the country's Independence Ceremony held on April 18. It was the greatest honour ever accorded the band, which underlined the Wailers' importance in the Third World.

However the concert itself was not without incident and was to have profound effects on Marley's feelings, not only about his beliefs, but also about his role as a campaigner for the Back to Africa movement.

The concert was held in the Rufaro Stadium in Salisbury, and outside the arena police had to use tear gas to control the crowds. Among the honoured guests at this historic event were the new Prime Minister Robert Mugabe and Prince Charles. The police and soldiers were worried because while Marley, the hero of black freedom fighters, was singing a huge mob was fighting to break into the arena. Eventually the police had to fire rifle shots over their heads and make baton charges. It wasn't exactly the kind of peace Bob had in mind, and he had to be led to safety during a 25-minute break, before the concert could resume.

The Marley who sang at what should have been one of the greatest moments in his life, was facing a personal crisis. His confidence in black African solidarity was being undermined, and he now had doubts about the significance of Haile Selassie. He was also suffering further pain in his right toe, but he had still refused to have it amputated.

Worse still, was the realization that perhaps his newly liberated audience in Zimbabwe, in the heat of the moment, weren't really listening to his music... or its message. There was much more work to do. But for Marley, time was running out.

> **"Herb like fruit. Keep you healthy, mind clear."**
> *Bob Marley explaining his theory of how to keep body and soul together in June 1976*

Redemption Song

In 1980 Bob Marley and the Wailers began work on a new album, called Uprising.

The Zimbabwe concert, for all its tensions and upsets, was still a very emotional experience for Bob Marley. Later he confirmed that he had enjoyed contributing to the celebrations and said: "It was strong, y'know. It was very nice. A good experience for me to take part in a thing like that. You feel a kind of solidarity with a lot of the people who were there. They support you more than just having the music. Other people will never really go through the experience, but them still become a part of it. People just want peace, justice and the right thing."

Marley was asked if he returned from the concert a changed man.

"You can say that again. But I really got the recharge from Ethiopia because that

song 'Zimbabwe' was written in a land called Shashamani in Ethiopia. So you can say it's a full re-charge. When the song came out it was a hit, so if you could write all your songs in Ethiopia, nearly every one would be a hit and somebody would say 'Boy, he is a prophet'."

In 1980 Bob Marley and the Wailers began work on their next album *Uprising*. It was released in May and was an instant hit, while the single from the LP, 'Could You Be Loved' was a world-wide best seller.

Uprising also featured 'Coming In From The Cold', 'Work' and the closing track 'Redemption Song'.

While work progressed on the album, visitors to the studios noticed that Bob had a strange aura about him—as if he was expecting the worst.

Marley had a strange aura about him. Sometimes he seemed to be expecting the worst.

Right: Bob, dreadlocks flying, played to capacity crowds throughout Europe in 1980.

Philosophical about success, money didn't concern the musician, who felt riches simply "made men foolish."

One day he told Junior Marvin who was about to depart from the studio: "Don't leave. Me don't have much time." Others noted that Marley was getting only two or three hours sleep a night.

Burn Down Babylon

Meanwhile Chris Blackwell came to hear the tapes for the new album and while he was impressed by a new song called 'Come We Go Burn Down Babylon (One More Time)' he asked Bob if he could come up with anything else. The next day Marley recorded the two extra songs 'Coming In From The Cold' and 'Redemption Song'.

Early in the year Marley visited American radio offices to help plan the breakthrough of the album. Since his success, he had long grown used to the idea of dealing with corporate rock moguls although he still didn't enjoy entering the glass and concrete towers of Babylon.

It was one of the contradictions he had to embrace as his fame pushed

Marley tried to keep fit, donning his track suit for jogging expeditions, during breaks in touring.

him into many strange situations that he'd never expected to encounter as a young man growing up in Trench Town.

He remained philosophical about the effects of fame and money on his life, which seemed to concern others more than himself.

Said Bob: "Money doesn't matter. Only music matters. When people think first about money and then about the music, the music won't be worth the money they were thinking about. I've always been successful from the beginning. It's like we come with success. I am success myself. I handle fame by not being famous…

I'm not famous to me. And once money spoil you, boy you ain't got no friends. Your friends is your money—that mean that all the people we have around like you, because you have money and then when our money is done, you're finished. You find most people, when they get money, they get withdrawn and foolish. Money is not my richness. My richness is to live and walk on the earth barefoot.

"I lived for a long time without money, but my work isn't aimed at becoming a star and I'm making sure my life don't go towards material vanity. I won't deny that at times I get a certain enjoyment out of success, but it's worldly enjoyment and I don't need it because it destroys you."

The Losing Battle

The Wailers started a major European tour, breaking capacity records throughout the continent. One of the shows was to a 100,000, capacity crowd in Milan—the biggest audience

Julian Marley—a chip off the old block.

Bob had played to in the Wailers' history. They were the hottest band on the road and the album was in every chart in Europe.

In a period of maximum excitement and optimism, plans were being made for an American tour with Stevie Wonder for the next winter.

At the end of the European tour Marley and the band went to America. Bob played two shows at Madison Square Garden, but immediately afterwards he was taken seriously ill.

He had been going jogging in Central Park, trying to keep fit, but he knew he was fighting a losing battle. The night after his second show at Madison Square, he awoke in a daze.

In 1980 Rita Marley had Bob baptized in the Ethiopian Orthodox Church, and he became a Christian Rasta.

"I hear the Police do something one time and I figure it kinda nice. It's not Jamaica it's coming from, but it still sound good."
Bob Marley September 1980

He had almost passed out during the performance and could barely remember what had happened.

The wound Marley had suffered three years earlier in Paris had turned cancerous and the disease was spreading through his entire body. If he had undergone the amputation of his toe earlier, he might have been saved—now it was too late.

Rita Marley called Bob's hotel from Pittsburgh to discover he had not checked in. Finally she was told he had been taken to a doctor and was said to have suffered from a stroke. She could not believe the news. When she finally met him, she could hardly recognise him because he had aged overnight.

Although Rita wanted to cancel the

tour, he was encouraged to do one more show. Some actually said it didn't make sense to cancel the tour, claiming "Bob is going to die anyway."

This callous view was not shared by Chris Blackwell and his lawyers. As soon as they heard Marley was seriously ill the tour was immediately cancelled.

Search For A Cure

There was also a clamp-down on press leaks and no one was to know that Marley was terminally ill. He was admitted to a Manhattan cancer hospital and underwent radium treatment that caused his famous dreadlocks to fall out. Radio reports finally revealed the truth, and as soon as it was known he was in hospital, the proud Rastaman checked out, ignoring his doctor's advice. It seemed the cancer had spread to his liver, lungs and brain but Bob was not going to give in. A Rastaman could not die.

Marley travelled to hospitals in

Bob Marley's final resting place.

The Bob Marley Museum serves to recall the highlights of his career.

Miami and then to a cancer clinic in Mexico, which had unsuccessfully treated movie star Steve McQueen. All the doctors he saw told him he was unlikely to see out the year.

On November 4, 1980, Rita had Bob baptized in the Ethiopian Orthodox Church, taking the name of Berhane Selassie and he became a Christian Rasta.

At this point a Jamaican doctor suggested that Bob seek the help of Dr Josef Issells, a 72-year-old German doctor who specialised in treating those with terminal cancer. Issells' treatment was controversial and non-toxic. The world was told that Marley was recovering from exhaustion in Ethiopia, while in fact by November he was in Issells' clinic in a small town in Bavaria, near the Austria border. He had grown depressed at stories circulating about his closeness to death and privacy became essential to keep up his spirits and increase his chances of survival.

The Last Moments

The medical community disparaged Issells' methods but he did manage to keep Marley alive for a further six months. By February 1981 Marley

Rita Marley became administrator of the Marley Estate.

seemed in good humour and he was able to get up and watch football on TV. But eventually the doctor announced that he could do no more and Marley was flown back to a hospital in Miami. Almost his final act was to insist that the publishing rights to his songs should be turned over to his family.

He died aged 36, only 40 hours after returning from Germany, just before noon on May 11, 1981.

A month before the end, Marley was awarded Jamaica's Order Of Merit, at the behest of the newly elected Prime Minister, Edward Seaga. As Bob was then ill in Germany, the award was accepted by Ziggy Marley in Kingston.

On Thursday May 21, 1981, the Hon. Robert Nesta Marley OM lay in state in Jamaica before an official funeral. Following a service that was

Ziggy Marley had a hit album with Play The Game Right.

Ex-Wailer Peter Tosh, who was murdered in September.

attended by both the Prime Minister and the Leader of the Opposition, Marley's body was taken to his birthplace at Nine Mile, on the north of the island, where the star now finally rests in a mausoleum.

The Marley Legend

Murder, litigation, battles over money, and the revelations that Marley himself had not been above strong arm tactics, could not destroy the pervading Marley magic. Whatever the truth about him, he had created great music, raised the esteem of a small, economically battered country and given its people a self-respect they might never otherwise have earned.

There was undoubtedly a dark side to Marley, mixed up in the hot conflicts of an Island in the Sun that few outside its realm really understood.

But what the world at large

Bob Marley—wreathed in glory.

Display at a 1991 Bob Marley travelling photo exhibition.

appreciated most was that Robert Nesta Marley was a special talent; that his music was both creative, innovative and deeply sincere. There were contradictions, and unanswered questions. But those who enjoy his music on its own merits, a dozen years after his death, are the true beneficiaries of the Marley legend.

"Man is a universe in himself."
Bob Marley was always more than just a singer—his life was lived according to a philosophy, a fragment revealed here in 1978

EPILOGUE

The Aftermath

Rita Marley, who inherited a large percentage of the Marley estate.

It was learned that the Marley estate was worth some $30 million and a large percentage of it went to his widow Rita Marley. Not unexpectedly, she began to enjoy a luxurious lifestyle and this was topped by her getting a hit single with 'One Draw', a song about ganja smoking feminists. She also had a hit album with *Who Feels It Knows It*. Rita cheerfully found herself becoming an international star and the self styled Queen of Reggae.

All the family made records, even Bob's mother, and it all seemed a long way from the grim edicts and poverty of the early days.

Ex-Wailer Peter Tosh, not to be outdone, had released a series of five solo albums, including some for Rolling Stones Records. The British rockers had constantly boosted his career until he fell out badly with Keith Richards and threatened to kill the Stones' peace loving guitarist.

The Melody Makers, featuring Ziggy Marley, had a hit album with *Play The Game Right* in 1985, released at the same time as Cedella Booker's LP *Redemption Songs*. Marley's mum became known as the Queen Mother of Reggae.

While attention was drawn to the heirs apparent, the legend of Marley lived on and the first posthumous album, *Confrontation*, appeared in 1983. He had begun work on it in 1980 and it had been planned as part of a trilogy, that began with *Survival* and *Uprising*. On the cover of the new album Bob was depicted as an Ethiopian horseman.

Winds Of Change

Reggae music in Jamaica was changing as new technology and fashions came in. Rap and Dub replaced the skills of the older musicians, and it was easier to be a toasting DJ than a master singer. It was unlikely there would ever be another reggae master in the mould of Bob Marley.

Another part of his legacy was the ongoing row over his estate and the Jamaican Supreme Court officially dismissed Rita Marley as estate administrator in 1987.

Although Bob Marley had always preached love and non-violence, his semi-Christian message had not always got through to the right people.

In a particularly gruesome incident, a posse of kidnappers abducted Aston and Carly Barrett's father. If a ransom had been demanded it must have been refused. Mr Barrett's decapitated and mutilated body was later found deep in the countryside.

Then, in April 1987, Carlton Barrett was murdered. His wife and her lover were later arrested and charged with the murder. The Wailers left Jamaica and toured the world to escape the atmosphere of death and madness. But it didn't stop there. In September 1987, Peter Tosh, the most successful ex-Wailer was a victim of Jamaican crime when he too was murdered.

Peter Tosh was murdered in 1987.

APPENDIX 1

Island in the sun

While he was at school Robert Marley had studied history with great interest, particularly the colonial story of his own country. Jamaica, set in the Caribbean Sea, was colonized by the Spanish from 1494, and they imported large numbers of Negro slaves. It was captured by the British in 1655 and became a colony in 1866, not gaining full independence until 1962. It was a member of the Commonwealth—its language English and its official religion Protestant.

As a British colony before Independence, Jamaica had been promoted as a tourist island, but despite its scenic splendour there was much poverty among the inhabitants. The sugar plantations provided some work, but for those living in the countryside the dream was to move to Jamaica's capital, Kingston.

Even when this was achieved, however, the ghetto's street youths, like Marley, were impatient and angry at their lowly place in the scheme of things. Although slavery had been abolished in 1834 its oppression and attack on the dignity of its victims had not been forgotten. Thus there was a distinctive mixture in Jamaican society of jealously preserved African traditions and British customs—quite unlike the experience of black African descendants in the more industrialized regions of America.

Garvey The Campaigner

Oppressed peoples naturally look towards a saviour or a leader who will help improve their conditions, and in the early years of the 20th Century a Jamaican preacher, Marcus Mosiah Garvey, began to formulate ideas about using the concept of a common African heritage. His political goals were given expression through the organisation he founded called the

Universal Negro Improvement Association (UNIA). The idea was to advocate the creation of a new black state in Africa, free of white domination.

Taking his first step to turn this dream into a reality, he founded the Black Star Line, a steamship company. One day, it was hoped, this company's liners would take the black populations of America and the Caribbean back to their African homelands. The cult of Rastafarianism, which Bob Marley would later propagate through his records, had its roots in Garvey's ideology.

Born in Jamaica in 1887, Garvey was a descendant of African slaves who had been released by the Spanish in 1655, before the island was invaded by Cromwell. He campaigned for black workers' rights and started his own newspaper. After travelling extensively around the Caribbean and South America he visited London in 1912 where he read an influential work of fiction called *Ethiopia Unbound* about black emancipation. It was this that inspired him to found UNIA on his return to Jamaica. Ironically he found that only enlightened white people would support his ideas, while the local population remained suspicious. He had to go to America to find encouragement and he campaigned for black pride with rallies at Madison Square Garden. His associates began to claim that a black king from Africa would be their redeemer.

Then in 1930 it seemed such prophecies had come true when Ras Tafari Makonnen was crowned Emperor of Ethiopia and took the formal title of Haile Selassie. The new Emperor claimed to be the 225th ruler in a line that stretched back to Menelik, the son of Solomon and Sheba.

The Black King

It seemed to Garvey's followers among the poor in Jamaica, consulting their New Testaments for a sign, that the Emperor was the saviour of the descendants of all the black Africans who had been displaced around the world. He was the black king whom Garvey had prophesied would deliver the Negro race.

It was the spark that encouraged the cult of Rastafarianism, although Garvey himself was apparently displeased with the Rasta Fari cult, which based its teachings on the Holy Piby—a "black man's bible."

Thus the new religion, which would later be espoused by Bob Marley in the Seventies, was established in Jamaica way back in the Thirties.

The cult established its own codes of practice on food and hygiene, and followers were urged not to eat meat and not to cut their hair. Rastafarians grew their hair into "dreadlocks," so called because of the dread inspired in those hostile to their bizarre appearance. As a child Bob Marley was considerably alarmed by the sight of the mysterious Rastas. It was also claimed that smoking copious amounts of ganja (marijuana) would improve the wisdom of true believers. There was an increasing clamour to have ganja made legal, and its open use by Rastafarians soon increased tension between them and the authorities both in Jamaica and England. But as Bob Marley would say later: "Herb like fruit. Keep you healthy, mind clear."

After the Second World War, during which Ethiopia had been invaded and occupied by the Italians, Haile Selassie returned to his throne and offered land to Jamaicans who had supported him during the period he spent in exile.

This all served to elevate his status and the Rastafarian movement began to expand, with rallies and even violent demonstrations throughout the Fifties and Sixties. Police action against the supporters only served to encourage the cult, and when Haile Selassie visited Jamaica in 1966 he was greeted by a crowd of 100,000 at the airport, eagerly awaiting the signal to rise up and then return to Africa.

The rest of the world, preoccupied with its own post-war problems, remained largely in ignorance of these tumultuous events until Bob Marley and the Wailers began to spread the word through reggae music. And the word was that according to Jah (Jehovah), Babylon (the world of the oppressors and exploiters), would surely fall. Such fiery preaching in the songs of the early reggae singers was greeted with alarm by the Establishment.

It is one of the ironies of the Marley saga, given the amount of government hostility towards the Rastafarians over many years, that just before Bob Marley's death he was awarded Jamaica's Order Of Merit, their third highest honour, in recognition of his outstanding contribution to the country's culture.

APPENDIX 2

Chris Blackwell — Gambling Man

Chris Blackwell's protegé—Bob Marley.

Chris Blackwell was a man who had an enormous influence on Bob Marley's career, even though he came from a wealthy background. Chris was born in London on June 22, 1937, to an Irish father who had family ties with the Crosse & Blackwell foodstuffs business. His mother Blanche Lindon was a descendant of Jamaican settlers who made their fortunes in the rum trade.

Blackwell was brought to Jamaica at the age of six months and lived there for nine years until he was sent to school in England, where he went to Harrow. After leaving public school he became an accountant—and a professional gambler!

He returned to Jamaica in 1958 to work as an aide to the Governor, Sir Hugh Foot. After running various businesses of his own he met author Ian Fleming who secured him a job working as an assistant to producer Harry Saltzman, on the first James Bond movie *Dr No* which was being filmed in Jamaica.

Blackwell might have pursued a career in the film industry, but after consulting a local fortune teller he decided to go into the record business. His subsequent success ensured he had a healthy respect for local magic.

Having grown up in Jamaica he had also got accustomed to the presence of the growing army of Rastafarians, so he could understand not only Bob Marley's patois, but the basis of his convictions.

In May 1962 Blackwell raised the money to launch Island Records as an outlet for Jamaican records in the UK. One of his earliest successes was with 15-year-old Millie whose bluebeat record 'My Boy Lollipop' was a huge international hit and sold six million copies in 1964. Among the records he re-issued in England in 1963 was Robert Marley's first single 'Judge Not', a fact which Marley recalled when the pair eventually met.

Blackwell went on to develop Island as an independent label after its early releases had been put out on Philips. He managed such UK bands as the Spencer Davis Group and went

on to launch a string of rock acts from Traffic to Free. He kept his ties with Jamaica, however, and signed artists like Jimmy Cliff, who starred in a movie called *The Harder They Fall*, about Jamaica's young outlaws. The title song from the movie was something of a flop, much to Jimmy Cliff's disappointment and he withdrew from the label, leaving the way clear for Bob Marley and the Wailers.

Impassioned Marley in full dreadlocked flow.

Discography

SINGLES:

1963: Judge Not; Do You Still Love Me
Island WI 088
Highest Chart Position:
— (UK) — (US)

1963: Exodus; One Cup of Coffee
Island WI 128
Highest Chart Position:
— (UK) — (US)

March 1965: It Hurts To Be Alone; Mr Talkative
Island WI 188
Highest Chart Position:
— (UK) — (US)

1965: Simmer Down; I Don't Need Your Love
Ska Beat JB186
Highest Chart Position:
— (UK) — (US)

August 1965: Play Boy; Your Love
Island WI 206
Highest Chart Position:
— (UK) — (US)

August 1965: Hoot Nanny Hoot; Do You Remember
Island WI 211
Highest Chart Position:
— (UK) — (US)

August 1965: Holligan; Maga Dog
Island WI 212
Highest Chart Position:
— (UK) — (US)

June 1965: Shame And Scandal; The Jerk
Island WI 215
Highest Chart Position:
— (UK) — (US)

June 1965: Don't Ever Leave Me; Donna
Island WI 216
Highest Chart Position:
— (UK) — (US)

1965: Lonesome Feelings; There She Goes
Ska Beat JB211
Highest Chart Position:
— (UK) — (US)

1965: Train to Ska-Ville; I Made a Mistake
Ska Beat JB226
Highest Chart Position:
— (UK) — (US)

1965: Love & Affection; Teenager In Love
Ska Beat JB228
Highest Chart Position:
— (UK) — (US)

January 1966: What's New Pussycat; Where Will I Find
Island WI 254
Highest Chart Position:
— (UK) — (US)

March 1966: Independent Anniversary Ska (I Should Have Known Better); Jumbie Jamboree
Island WI 260
Highest Chart Position:
— (UK) — (US)

March 1966: Put It On; Love Won't Be Mine

Island WI 268
Highest Chart Position:
— (UK) — (US)

1966: And I Love Her; Do It Right
Ska Beat JB230
Highest Chart Position:
— (UK) — (US)

1966: Lonesome Track; Zimmerman
Ska Beat JB249
Highest Chart Position:
— (UK) — (US)

July 1966: Rude Boy/Ringo's Theme (This Boy)
Doctor Bird DB1013
Highest Chart Position:
— (UK) — (US)

1966: Good Good Rudie; Oceans 11
Doctor Bird DB1021
Highest Chart Position:
— (UK) — (US)

November 1966: He Who Feels It Knows It; Sunday Morning
Island WI 3001
Highest Chart Position:
— (UK) — (US)

1966: Come By Here; I Stand Predominate

Studio 1 SO2024
Highest Chart Position:
— (UK) — (US)

1966: Rasta Put It On; Ska With Ringo
Doctor Bird DB1039
Highest Chart Position:
— (UK) — (US)

December 1966: Let Him Go (Rude Boy Get Bail); Sinner Man
Island WI 3009
Highest Chart Position:
— (UK) — (US)

1966: Dancing Shoes; Don't Look Back
Rio R116
Highest Chart Position:
— (UK) — (US)

1967: I Am The Toughest; No Faith
Island WI 3042
Highest Chart Position:
— (UK) — (US)

April 1967: Bend Down Low; Freedom Time
Island WI 3043
Highest Chart Position:
— (UK) — (US)

1967: Nice Time; Hypocrite
Doctor Bird DB1091

Highest Chart Position:
— (UK) — (US)

October 1968: Stir It
Up; This Train
Trojan TR617
Highest Chart Position:
— (UK) — (US)

1970: Stranger In
Love; Jailhouse
Bamboo BAM55
Highest Chart Position:
— (UK) — (US)

1970: To The Rescue;
Run For Cover
Escort ERT842
Highest Chart Position:
— (UK) — (US)

September 1970: Soul
Shake Down Party;
Shake Down Version
Trojan TR7759
Highest Chart Position:
— (UK) — (US)

1970: My Cup; Son of
Thunder
Upsetter US340
Highest Chart Position:
— (UK) — (US)

1970: Dreamland;
Version of Cup
Upsetter US342
Highest Chart Position:

— (UK) — (US)

October 1970: Duppy
Conqueror; Justice
Upsetter US348
Highest Chart Position:
— (UK) — (US)

1970: Duppy
Conqueror; Justice
Unity UN562
Highest Chart Position:
— (UK) — (US)

1970: Upsetting
Station; Dig Your Grave
Upsetter US349
Highest Chart Position:
— (UK) — (US)

January 1971: Mr
Brown; Dracula
Upsetter US354
Highest Chart Position:
— (UK) — (US)

February 1971: Kaya;
Version
Upsetter US356
Highest Chart Position:
— (UK) — (US)

February 1971: Small
Axe; All In One
Upsetter US357
Highest Chart Position:
— (UK) — (US)

1971: Small Axe;

What A Confusion
Punch PH69
Highest Chart Position:
— (UK) — (US)

1971: Down Presser;
Got The Tip
Punch PH77
Highest Chart Position:
— (UK) — (US)

1971: I Like It Like
This; Am Sorry
Supreme SUP216
Highest Chart Position:
— (UK) — (US)

1971: Soultown; Let
The Sun Shine On Me
Bullet BU464
Highest Chart Position:
— (UK) — (US)

1971: Picture On The
Wall; Picture Version
Upsetter US368
Highest Chart Position:
— (UK) — (US)

1971: More Axe; The
Axe Man
Upsetter US369
Highest Chart Position:
— (UK) — (US)

1971: Dreamland;
Dream Version
Upsetter US371

Highest Chart Position:
— (UK) — (US)

1971: More Axe; The
Axe Man
Upsetter US372
(recording the same as
US369)
Highest Chart Position:
— (UK) — (US)

November 1971:
Trench Town Rock;
Grooving Kingston 12
Green Door GD4005
Highest Chart Position:
— (UK) — (US)

1971: Lick Samba;
Samba Version
Bullet BU493
Highest Chart Position:
— (UK) — (US)

1971: Mr Chatterbox;
Walk Through the
World
Jackpot JP730
Highest Chart Position:
— (UK) — (US)

1971: Stop The Train;
Caution
Summit SUM8526
Highest Chart Position:
— (UK) — (US)

1971: Let The Lord Be

Seen In You; White
Christmas
Supreme
Highest Chart Position:
— (UK) — (US)

1972: Lively Up
Yourself; Live
Green Door GD4022
Highest Chart Position:
— (UK) — (US)

1972: Guava Jelly;
Redder Then Red
Green Door GD4025
Highest Chart Position:
— (UK) — (US)

May 1972: Reggae on
Broadway; Oh Lord I
Got To Get There
CBS8144
Highest Chart Position:
— (UK) — (US)

1972: You Should
Have Known Better;
Known Better
Punch PH114
Highest Chart Position:
(UK) — (US)

September 1972: Keep
On Moving; African
Herbsman
Upsetter US392
Highest Chart Position:
—(UK) — (US)

113

1972: Screw Face; Face Man
Punch PH101
Highest Chart Position: —(UK) — (US)

January 1973: Baby Baby We've Got A Date; Stop That Train
Blue Mountain BM1021
Highest Chart Position: —(UK) — (US)

June 1973: Concrete Jungle; Reincarnated Soul
Island WI6164
Highest Chart Position: —(UK) — (US)

September 1973: Get Up Stand Up; Slave Driver
Island WIP6167
Highest Chart Position: —(UK) — (US)

November 1973: I Shot The Sheriff; Pass It On; Duppy Conqueror
Island IDJ2
Highest Chart Position: — (UK) — (US)

1974: Soul Shakedown Party; Caution
Trojan TR7911

Highest Chart Position: — (UK) — (US)

August 1974: Mr Brown; Version
Trojan TR7926
Highest Chart Position: — (UK) — (US)

1974: So Jah Seh; Natty Dread
Island WIP6212
Highest Chart Position: — (UK) — (US)

1975: Trenchtown Rock; I Shot The Sheriff
Island IDJ7
Highest Chart Position: — (UK) — (US)

27 Sept 1975: No Woman No Cry; Kinky Reggae
Island WIP6244
Highest Chart Position: 22 (UK) — (US)

January 1976: Jah Live; Concrete
Island WIP6265
Highest Chart Position: — (UK) — (US)

April 1976: Johnny Was (Woman Hold Her Head and Cry); Cry To

Me
Island WIP6296
Highest Chart Position: — (UK) — (US)

June 1976: Roots Rock Reggae; Stir It Up
Island WIP6309
Highest Chart Position: —(UK) 51 (US)

1976: Mr Brown; Trenchtown Rock
Trojan TR7979
Highest Chart Position: — (UK) — (US)

January 1977: Reggae On Broadway; Oh Lord I Got To Get There
CBS4902
Highest Chart Position: — (UK) — (US)

25 June 1977: Exodus; Instrumental
Island WIP6390
Highest Chart Position: 14 (UK) — (US)

10 September 1977: Waiting In Vain; Roots
Island WIP6402
Highest Chart Position: 27 (UK) — (US)

10 December 1977: Jamming; Punky

Reggae Party
Island WIP6410
Highest Chart Position: 9 (UK) — (US)

25 February 1978: Is This Love; Crisis (Version)
Island WIP6420
Highest Chart Position: 9 (UK) — (US)

10 June 1978: Satisfy My Soul; Smile Jamaica
Island WIP6440
Highest Chart Position: 21 (UK) — (US)

1978: War; No More Trouble
Island IPR2026
Highest Chart Position: — (UK) — (US)

January 1979: Stir It Up; Rat Race
Island WIP6478
Highest Chart Position: — (UK) — (US)

20 October 1979: So Much Trouble In The World; Instrumental
Island WIP6510
Highest Chart Position: 56 (UK) — (US)

November 1979: Survival; Wake Up and Live
Island WIP6553
Highest Chart Position: — (UK) — (US)

March 1980: Zimbabwe; Survival
Island WIP6597
Highest Chart Position: —(UK) — (US)

March 1980: Zimbabwe; Africa Unite; Wake Up and Live
Island 12WIP6597
Highest Chart Position: — (UK) — (US)

21 June 1980: Could You Be Loved; One Drop
Island WIP6610
Highest Chart Position: 21 (UK) — (US)

May 1980: Could You Be Loved; One Drop; Ride Natty Ride
Island 12WIP6610
Highest Chart Position: — (UK) — (US)

13 September 1980: Three Little Birds; Every Need Got An

Ego To Feed
Island WIP6641
Highest Chart Position:
17 (UK) — (US)

October 1980:
Redemption Song;
Redemption Song
(Band version)
Island WIP6653
Highest Chart Position:
— (UK) — (US)

October 1980:
Redemption Song;
Redemption Song
(Band version); I Shot
The Sheriff
Island 12WIP6653
Highest Chart Position:
— (UK) — (US)

June 1981: Thank You
Lord; Wisdom
Trojan TRO9065
Highest Chart Position:
— (UK) — (US)

13 June 1981: No
Woman No Cry;
Jamming
Island 12WIP6244
Highest Chart Position:
8 (UK) — (US)

September 1981:
Reggae On Broadway;
Gonna Get You

Warner K79250
Highest Chart Position:
— (UK) — (US)

March 8, 1982: Natural
Mystic; Carry Us
Beyond
Island WIP6774
Highest Chart Position:
— (UK) — (US)

7 May 1983: Buffalo
Soldier; Buffalo Dub
Island IS108
Highest Chart Position:
4 (UK) — (US)

October 1983: Soul
Shakedown Party;
Caution
Trojan TROT9074
Highest Chart Position:
— (UK) — (US)

21 April 1984: One
Love; People Get
Ready; So Much
Trouble In The World
Island IS169
Highest Chart Position:
5 (UK) — (US)

April 9 1984: One
Love; People Get
Ready(extended
version); So Much
Trouble In The World;
Keep On Moving

Island 12IS169
Highest Chart Position:
— (UK) — (US)

23 June 1984: Waiting
In Vain; Black Man
Redemption
Island IS180
Highest Chart Position:
31 (UK) — (US)

1984: Waiting In Vain;
Black Man Redemption;
Marley Mix Up (a
Exodus, b Positive
Vibration, c Pimpers
Paradise, d Punky
Reggae Party
Island 12IS180
Highest Chart Position:
— (UK) — (US)

8 December 1984:
Could You Be Loved;
Jamming; No Woman
No Cry; Coming In
From The Cold
Island 12IS210
Highest Chart Position:
71 (UK) — (US)

ALBUMS:

December 1970: Soul
Rebels
Trojan TBL126
Highest Chart Position:
— (UK) — (US)

1973: African
Herbsman
Trojan TRLS62
Highest Chart Position:
— (UK) — (US)

April 1973: Catch A
Fire
Island ILPS9241
Highest Chart Position:
— (UK)/ November
1976 171 (US)

November 1973:
Burnin'
Island ILPS9256
Highest Chart Position:
— (UK) —October
1975 151 (US)

July 1974: Rasta
Revolution
Trojan TRLS89
Highest Chart Position:
— (UK) — (US)

4 October 1975: Natty
Dread
Island ILPS9281
Highest Chart Position:
43 (UK)/ May 1975 99
(US)

20 December 1975:
Live At The Lyceum
Island ILPS9376
Highest Chart Position:
— (UK) — (US)

80 (US)

8 May 1976: Rastaman
Vibration
Island ILPS9383
Highest Chart Position:
15 (UK) May 1976 8
(US)

11 June 1977: Exodus
Island ILPS9498
Highest Chart Position:
8 (UK) June 1977 20
(US)

1977: The Birth Of A
Legend
Epic 82066
Highest Chart Position:
—(UK) — (US)

1977: Early Music
Epic 82067
Highest Chart Position:
— (UK) — (US)

1 April 1978: Kaya
Island ILPS9517
Highest Chart Position:
4 (UK) April 1978 50
(US)

16 December 1978:
Babylon By Bus
(Double)
Island ISLD11
Highest Chart Position:
40 (UK)/ December

1978 102 (US)

13 October 1979:
Survival
Island ILPS9542
Highest Chart Position:
20 (UK) November
1979 70 (US)

October 1979: In The
Beginning
Psycho PLP6002
Highest Chart Position:
— (UK) — (US)

October 1979: Bob
Marley And The Wailers
Hammer HMR9006
Highest Chart Position:
— (UK) — (US)

28 June 1980: Uprising
Island ILPS9596
Highest Chart Position:
6 (UK) August 1980
45 (US)

September 1981: Bob
Marley And The Wailers
With Peter Tosh
Hallmark SHM3048
Highest Chart Position:
— (UK) — (US)

September 1981: Soul
Rebel
New Cross NC001
Highest Chart Position:

— (UK) — (US)

1981: Bob Marley And
The Wailers
SS International SSS35
Highest Chart Position:
— (UK) — (US)

1981: Jamaican Storm
Accord SN7211
Highest Chart Position:
— (UK) — (US)

October 1981:
Chances Are
WEA K99183
Highest Chart Position:
(UK) Cotillion October
1981 117 (US)

1982: Riding High
Everest CBR1004
Highest Chart Position:
— (UK) — (US)

28 May 1983:
Confrontation
Island ILPS9760
Highest Chart Position:
5 (UK) July 1983 55
(US)

January 1984: In The
Beginning
Trojan TRLS221
Highest Chart Position:
— (UK) — (US)

19 May 1984: Legend

Island BMW1
Highest Chart Position:
1 (UK)/ August 1984
54 (US)

28 July 1986: Rebel
Music
Island 90520
Highest Chart Position:
54 (UK)/ June 1986
140 (US)

CD LISTING:

August 1985: Legend
Island CID 103

September 1986: Live
At The Lyceum
Island CID 114

1986: Rebel Music
Island CID 9843

January 1987: Exodus
Island CID 9498

January 1987: Live At
The Lyceum
Island CID 9376

February 1987:
Babylon By Bus
Island CIDD 11

February 1987: Kaya
Island CID 9517

February 1987:
Uprising
Island CID 9596

April 1987: Mellow
Mood
Topline TOP CD 505

April 1987: Natty Dread
Island CID 9281

April 1987: Rastaman
Vibration
Island CID 9383

April 1987: Survival
Island CID 9542

June 1988: African
Herbsman
Trojan CDTRL 62

June 1988: In The
Beginning
Trojan CDTRL 221

June 1988: Rasta
Revolution
Trojan CDTRL 89

June 1988: Soul
Revolution I & II
Trojan CDTRD 406

September 1988:
Reaction
Pickwick PWK 072

November 1988:
Classic Tracks
Classic Tracks CD
Single CDEP 3 C

1988: Bob, Peter,
Bunny & Rita
Metronome 827 007 2

1988: Collection: Bob
Marley
Castle Collector Series
CCSCD 123

1988: Confrontation
CID 9760

1988: One Love
Pickwick PWK 002

1988: Roots
Blue Moon CDTB 1032

1989: One Love/Roots
Vol 2
Roots Records CDBM
1052

April 1990: Soul Rebel
Action Replay CDAR
1013

June 1990: Best of Bob
Marley (1968-1972)
Connoisseur Collection
CSAPCD 107

June 1990: Burnin'
Tuff Gong RRCD 2

June 1990: Catch A
Fire
Tuff Gong RRCD 1

June 1990: Natty
Dread
Tuff Gong RRCD 3

June 1990: Rebel
Music
Tuff Gong RRCD 5

November 1990:
Babylon By Bus
Island TGDCD 1

November 1990:
Exodus
Island TGLCD 6

November 1990: Kaya
Island TGLCD 7

November 1990: Live:
Bob Marley
Island TGLCD 4

November 1990:
Survival
Island TGLCD 9

November 1990:
Rastaman Vibration
Island TGLCD 5

November 1990:
Uprising
Island TGLCD 9

1990: Confrontation
Tuff Gong RRCD 4

February 1991: Talkin'
Blues
Tuff Gong TGLCD 12
Highest Chart Position:
(UK) — February 1991
103 (US)

April 1991: All The Hits
Rohit RRTGCD 7757

May 1991: In
Memoriam
Trojan CDTAL 400

May 1991: Legend
Island BMWCD 1

May 1991: One Love -
People Get Ready
Tuff Gong TGX CD 1

June 1991: The Birth
Of A Legend
Pickwick 9825882

August 1991: Saga
Enteleky UCD 19026

September 1991: Very
Best Of The Early
Years

Music Club MCCD 033

November 1991: One
Love
Special Delivery HB
111 CD

1991: Reggae Roots
BMG 901622

March 1992: His 24
Greatest Hits
Entertainers ENT CD
282

June 1992: Audio
Archive
Tring CDAA 047

June 1992: Nice Time
Creole REG 115

August 1992: Bob
Marley And The Wailers
(Upsetter Record Shop
PL1)
Rhino LG 21040

August 1992: Bob
Marley And The
Wailers (Upsetter
Record Shop PL2)
Rhino LG 21044

September 1992: Iron
Lion Zion
Tuff Gong TGXCD 2

September 1992:
Songs of Freedom
Tuff Gong TGCBX 1
Highest Chart Position:
(UK) —October 1992
86 (US)

October 1992: Keep
On Moving
Pickwick SMS 030

October 1992: The
Legendary
Pickwick SMD 32

October 1992: Soul
Almighty
Pickwick SMS 52

October 1992: Stir It
Up
Pickwick SMS 04

November 1992: The
Best
Laserlight 15 499

November 1992: Why
Should I
Tuff Gong TGXCD - 3

December 1992:
Natural Mystic
Avid AVC 506

1992: 16 Greatest Hits
Point (2) 26 20 092

1992: Kinky Reggae
Dillion 26 10 012

1992: Lively Up
Yourself
Dillion 26 10 022

1992: Rainbow
Country
Dillion 26 10 032

May 1993: Lively Up
Yourself
Prestige CDSGP 056

July 1993: Soul Rebel
Receiver RRCD 106

Chronology

1945 February 6 Robert Nesta Marley is born
1947 April 10 Neville Livingstone is born
1955 May 20 Norval Marley dies
1963 Bob Marley forms the Wailers (first named the Teenagers)
1963 December Bob Marley and the Wailers release their first single 'Simmer Down'
1966 February 10 Bob Marley and Rita Anderson marry
1973 Bob Marley and the Wailers tour England and America
1975 October 11 Bob Marley and the Wailers play in Kingston
1976 December Bob Marley and the Wailers play at the Smile Jamaica concert

1976 December An assassination attempt on Bob Marley fails leaving him with a bullet wound in the arm
1977 May Bob Marley injures his right toe playing football with a French team
1978 April 22 Bob Marley plays at the Love Peace concert in Jamaica
1979 Bob Marley forms the Melody Makers with his family
1979 September 24 Bob Marley plays at the National Heroes Arena for Rasta children
1980 April 18 Bob Marley and the Wailers Play at an Independence Ceremony after Rhodesia declares Independance under the new name of Zimbabwe

1980 November 4 Bob Marley is baptized in the Ethiopian Orthodox Church
1981 May 11 Bob Marley dies of cancer from his untreated toe
1981 May 21 Bob Marley's funeral is held. Following this, Ziggy Marley accepts Jamaica's Order of Merit on his father's behalf
1987 September Peter McIntosh is murdered

Picture Acknowledgements

Photographs reproduced by kind permission of **London Features International**; **Pictorial Press**/Bob Gruen,/Brian Rasic; **Retna Pictures**/Adrian Boot,/Ray Burmiston,/Kevin Cummins Front cover picture: London Features International

Index